QUICK GUIDE TO THE APA REFERENCING STYLE

Easy Steps to Format Your Paper

PaperHacker Publications

HEADER

Title Page

Running head is a shortened version of the paper:
- Maximum 50 characters, including spaces and punctuation; UPPERCASE and flush left; font: Times New Roman, 12pt.

Example:
Running head: HOW TO FORMAT ACADEMIC PAPER IN APA STYLE
Before the shortened title, there are words "Running head." It is used to help readers identify the titles for the published articles (even if your paper is not indented for publication, your paper should still have a running head).

Other Pages

- On the title page, the running head should include the words "Running head:"
- For pages following the title page, repeat the running head in all caps without "Running head:"
- Shortened paper title should appear on the rest of the pages but not include the words "Running head:"

Example:
HOW TO FORMAT ACADEMIC PAPER IN APA STYLE

Page Numbers

- Page number is included on the first page.
- It is flush right.
- Font: Times New Roman 12pt.

TITLE PAGE

- Title page contains the title of the paper, author's name and institution formatted in Times New Roman 12 pt font, centered, regular typed and double-spaced.

Example:

Formatting Academic Paper in APA Style
Student
Institution
Date

The title should summarize the paper's main idea and identify the variables under discussion and the relationship between them. The author's name and the institution should be double-spaced and centered.

ABSTRACT

The Abstract is a summary of the paper, allowing the readers to review the main points and the purpose of the article quickly. The abstract should be **150-250 words long**. Abbreviations and acronyms used in the paper should be defined in the abstract. It should be placed on a separate page and be entitled "Abstract" (regular type and centered).

You may also list keywords from your paper there. Indent this section as for a new paragraph. Keywords: (italicized), and then list your keywords with no dot at the end.

Example:

Abstract

Text of your abstract containing 150-250 words.
Do not intend any paragraph of your abstract.
    Keywords: APA format, APA style, abstract

INTRODUCTION & MAIN CONTENT

The title should be centered on the page, not bolded, typed in 12-point Times New Roman Font. It should not be bolded, underlined, or italicized. The introduction (Heading 1 Level) presents the problem that the paper addresses.

Example:

Formatting Academic Paper in APA Style

Introduction

HEADINGS

Level 1 Heading

Level 1 heading is bolded, centered, and title case.

Example:

How to Cite Sources in APA Citation Format
Text.

Level 2 Heading

Level 2 heading should be flush with the left margin, bolded, and title case.

Example:

How to Cite Sources in APA Citation Format
Text.

Level 3 Heading

Level 3 heading should indent 0.5" from the left margin, bolded and lower case (except for the first word). The text should follow immediately after.

Example:

How to cite sources in APA citation format. Text.

Example

The Title of Paper
First Level

Lorem ipsum dolor sit amet, porro ullum ne sea, ad vis odio decore. Ne corrumpit iracundia pri. Euismod hendrerit repudiandae nec at.

Second Level

Lorem ipsum dolor sit amet, porro ullum ne sea, ad vis odio decore. Ne corrumpit gubergren referrentur nec, sed cu quot causae sententiae. Quodsi eleifend pri ut. Ei lobortis iracundia pri. Euismod hendrerit repudiandae nec at.

Third level. Lorem ipsum dolor sit amet, porro ullum ne sea, ad vis odio decore. Ne corrumpit gubergren referrentur nec, sed cu quot causae sententiae. Quodsi eleifend pri ut. Ei lobortis iracundia pri. Euismod hendrerit repudiandae nec at.

Fourth level. Lorem ipsum dolor sit amet, porro ullum ne sea, ad vis odio decore. Ne lobortis iracundia pri. Euismod hendrerit repudiandae nec at.

Fifth level. Lorem ipsum dolor sit amet, porro ullum ne sea, ad vis odio decore. Ne lobortis iracundia pri. Euismod hendrerit repudiandae nec at.

BODY

Papers entailing field research, where you set up a study and collect data, should include the following sections:

(1) Introduction

- This section prepares the reader for what is to come.
- Introduce reader to the topic/problem under discussion.
- State why it is important to discuss.
- State briefly what is already known about this topic.
- State very briefly how the topic will be explored in this paper.
- State the main claim (hypothesis) that is made about the topic.

(2) Literature review

This section is focused on setting the stage for research. It should offer the following:
- A summary of the literature devoted to the topic.
- Conclusions drawn on the topic so far.
- The need for further research revealed by this review.

(3) Methods

This section provides the reader with details about how the research was conducted. It may include information about research subjects and materials used.

(4) Results

This section presents the results of the research. It is different from the Discussion section in that the results are not analyzed, but simply reported.

(5) Discussion

This section analyzes the research results.

(6) Conclusion

This section reviews the major points of the paper and paraphrases the information in the introduction:

- It reminds the readers what they have just learned.
- Reiterates the topic/problem discussed.
- States the importance of the findings.
- Summarizes the main findings of the research.
- Leaves the reader with a final thought or recommendation.

TABLES

Table Structure

- **Numbers.** Number all tables with Arabic numerals sequentially. Do not use suffix letters (e.g. Table 3a, 3b, 3c); instead, combine the related tables. If the manuscript includes an appendix with tables, identify them with capital letters and Arabic numerals (e.g. Table A1, Table B2).
- **Titles.** Like the title of the paper itself, each table must have a clear and concise title. When appropriate, you may use the title to explain an abbreviation parenthetically.

Example:

Comparison of Median Income of Adopted Children (AC) v. Foster Children (FC)

- **Headings.** Keep headings clear and brief. The heading should not be much wider than the widest entry in the column. Use of standard abbreviations can aid in achieving that goal. All columns must have headings, even the stub column, which customarily lists the major independent variables.

Example

Table 1
Title
Header

Subhead	Column Head	Column Head	Column Head
Row name	X	X	X
Row name	X	X	X
Row name	X	X	X
Row name	X	X	X

Table 1

FIGURES

- For figures, make sure to include the figure number and a title with a legend and caption. These elements appear below the visual display. For the figure number, type Figure X. Then type the title of the figure in sentence case. Follow the title with a legend that explains the symbols in the figure and a caption that explains the figure.

Example:

Figure 1. How to create figures in APA style. This figure illustrates effective elements in APA style figures.

- Captions serve as a brief, but complete, explanation and as a title. For example, "*Figure 4.* Population" is insufficient, whereas "*Figure 4.* Population of Grand Rapids, MI by race (1980)" is better. If the figure has a title in the image, crop it.

IN-TEXT CITING

General

- APA requires you to include the publication year because APA users are concerned with the date of the article (the more current, the better).
- In-text citations that are direct quotes should include the author's/authors' name/s, the publication year, and page number/s.

Example:

According to Jones (1998), "Students often had difficulty using APA style, especially when it was their first time" (p. 199).

- In-text citations to books with more than one author contain mark '&' between the surnames).

Example:
(Berry & Harlow, 1993)

- If an article has three to five authors, write out all of the authors' names the first time they appear. Then use the first author's last name, followed by "et al."

Example:

First time: (Kernis, Cornell, Sun, Berry, & Harlow, 1993)
Then: (Kernis et al., 1993)

Short Quotations

- If you are directly quoting from a work, you will need to include the author, year of publication, and page number for the reference (preceded by "p."). Introduce the quotation with a signal phrase that includes the author's last name followed by the date of publication in parentheses.

Example:

According to Jones (1998), "Students often had difficulty using APA style, especially when it was their first time" (p. 199).

Jones (1998) found "students often had difficulty using APA style" (p. 199); what implications does this have for teachers?

- If the author is not named in a signal phrase, place the author's last name, the year of publication, and the page number in parentheses after the quotation.

Example:

She stated, "Students often had difficulty using APA style" (Jones, 1998, p. 199), but she did not offer an explanation as to why.

Long Quotations

- Place direct quotations that are 40 words or longer in a free-standing block of typewritten lines and omit quotation marks. Start the quotation on a new line, indented 1/2 inch from the left margin, i.e., in the same place you would begin a new paragraph. Type the entire quotation on the new margin, and indent the first line of any subsequent paragraph within the quotation 1/2 inch from the new margin. Maintain double-spacing throughout. The parenthetical citation should come after the closing punctuation mark.

Example:

Jones's (1998) study found the following:

> Students often had difficulty using APA style, especially when it was their first time citing sources. This difficulty could be attributed to the fact that many students failed to purchase a style manual or to ask their teacher for help. (p. 199)

Summary or Paraphrase

- If you are paraphrasing an idea from another work, you only have to make reference to the author and year of publication in your in-text reference, but APA guidelines encourage you to also provide the page number (although it is not required).

Example:

According to Jones (1998), APA style is a difficult citation format for first-time learners.

APA style is a difficult citation format for first-time learners (Jones, 1998, p. 199).

REFERENCES

- References page should be entitled "Reference(s)" (regular type and centered).
- The references should appear on a separate page.
- References should be listed in alphabetical order and include the details required for each type of source.
- The references page appears at the end of the document before appendices.
- The list of references should account for all in-text citations.
- All entries must be placed with a hanging indent, so that the first line is flushed left and subsequent lines are indented.

AUTHORS

Single Author

- Last name first, followed by author initials.

Example:

Berndt, T. J. (2002). Friendship quality and social development. *Current Directions in Psychological Science, 11*, 7-10.

Two Authors

- List by their last names and initials. Use the ampersand instead of "and."

Example:

Wegener, D. T., & Petty, R. E. (1994). Mood management across affective states: The hedonic contingency hypothesis. *Journal of Personality and Social Psychology, 66*, 1034-1048.

Three to Seven Authors

- List by last names and initials; commas separate author names, while the last author name is preceded again by ampersand.

Example:

Kernis, M. H., Cornell, D. P., Sun, C. R., Berry, A., Harlow, T., & Bach, J. S. (1993). There's more to self-esteem than whether it is high or low: The importance of stability of self-esteem. *Journal of Personality and Social Psychology, 65*, 1190-1204.

More than Seven Authors

- List by last names and initials; commas separate author names. After the sixth author's name, use an ellipsis in place of the author names. Then provide the final author name. There should be no more than seven names.

Example:

Miller, F. H., Choi, M. J., Angeli, L. L., Harland, A. A., Stamos, J. A., Thomas, S. T., . . . Rubin, L. H. (2009). Web site usability for the blind and low-vision user. *Technical Communication, 57,* 323-335.

Organization as Author

- Also known as a "corporate author." Here, you simply treat the publishing organization the same way you would treat the author's name and format the rest of the citation as normal.

Example:

American Psychological Association. (2009). Blog guidelines. *APA Style Blog.* Retrieved from https://blog.apa-style.org/apastyle/blog-guidelines.html

Unknown Author

Example:

Merriam-Webster's collegiate dictionary (10th ed.). (1993). Springfield, MA: Merriam-Webster.

- When your essay includes parenthetical citations of sources with no author named, use a shortened version of the source's title instead of an author's name. Use quotation marks and italics as appropriate. For example, parenthetical citations of the source above would appear as follows: (*Merriam-Webster's,* 1993).

BOOKS

General Format:

Author, A. A. (Year of publication). *Title of work: Capital letter also for subtitle.* Location: Publisher.

Example:

Calfee, R. C., & Valencia, R. R. (1991). *APA guide to preparing manuscripts for journal publication.* Washington, DC: American Psychological Association.

ARTICLES

Article in Periodicals

General Format:

Author, A. A., Author, B. B., & Author, C. C. (Year). Title of article. *Title of Periodical, volume number*(issue number), pages. https://doi.org/xx.xxx/yyyy

Example:

Scruton, R. (1996). The eclipse of listening. *The New Criterion, 15*(3), 5-13.

Article from an Online Periodical

- Online articles follow the same guidelines for printed articles. Include all information the online host makes available, including an issue number in parentheses.

General Format:

Author, A. A., & Author, B. B. (Date of publication). Title of article. *Title of Online Periodical, volume number*(issue number if available). Retrieved from https://www.someaddress.com/full/url/

Example:

Bernstein, M. (2002). 10 tips on writing the living web. *A List Apart: For People Who Make Websites, 149*. Retrieved from https://www.alistapart.com/articles/writeliving

Article from an Online Periodical with no DOI Assigned

- Online scholarly journal articles without a DOI require the URL of the journal home page. Remember that one goal of citations is to provide your readers with enough information to find the article; providing the journal home page aids readers in this process.

General Format:

Author, A. A., & Author, B. B. (Date of publication). Title of article. *Title of Journal, volume number*(issue number if available). Retrieved from https://www.journalhomepage.com/full/url/

Article from an Online Periodical with DOI Assigned

General Format:

Author, A. A., & Author, B. B. (Date of publication). Title of article. *Title of Journal, volume number*(issue number if available), page range. doi:0000000/000000000000 or https://doi.org/10.0000/0000

Example:

Brownlie, D. (2007). Toward effective poster presentations: An annotated bibliography. *European Journal of Marketing, 41,* 1245-1283. doi:10.1108/03090560710821161

WEBPAGE CONTENT

General Format:

Author, A. A. & Author B. B. (Date of publication). Title of page [Format description when necessary]. Retrieved from https://www.someaddress.com/full/url/

Example:

Eco, U. (2015). How to write a thesis [PDF file]. (Farina C. M. & Farina F., Trans.) Retrieved from https://www.research-gate.net/...How_to_write_a_thesis/.../Umberto+Eco-How+to+Write+... (Original work published 1977).

- If the page's author is not listed, start with the title instead. If the date of publication is not listed, use the abbreviation (n.d.).

Example:

Spotlight Resources. (n.d.). Retrieved from https://owl.purdue.edu/owl/about_the_owl/owl_information/spotlight_resources.html

QUICK GUIDE ON REFERENCES EXAMPLES

Book: 1 or 2 authors

Peters, S. N., & Abbott, M. R. (2001). *Canadian parliamentary law: A call for change.* Toronto, ON: Carswell.

Book: 3 to 7 authors

Smith, K., Jones, M., & Andrews, O. (2005). *Guide to Canadian historical sites for families.* Ottawa, ON: Penguin.

Book: 8 or more authors

Kernis, M., Cornell, D., Sun, C., Berry, A., Harlow, T., Ball, E., . . . Bach, J. (2012). *Cooperative endeavors in science education.* New York, NY: Random House.

Book: group as author (agency, organization, company, etc.)

Canadian Mental Health Association. (2007). *Mental health indicators for adolescents.* Ottawa, Canada: Canadian Mental Health Association.

First in-text citation:
(Canadian Mental Health Association [CMHA], 2003)

Subsequent citations:
(CMHA, 2003)

Book: no author

Merriam-Webster's geographical dictionary (3 rd ed.). (1997). Springfield, MA: Merriam-Webster.

Book: with editor(s)

Allen, S., & Graham, P. (Eds.). (2005). *Contemporary studies in romance languages.* New York, NY: McGraw Hill.

Book, edited: chapter or article

Store, W. (2003). The Doane ukulele method. In T. Miller & L. E. Davis (Eds.), *Music education in Canada* (4th ed., pp. 197–203). St. Catharines, ON: Vanwell.

Book, edition other than first

Craig, B., & Germain, D. (2014). *Abnormal Psychology* (5th ed.). Chicago, IL: University of Chicago Press.

Book: retrieved from a database (no direct link)

Erdkamp, P. (2005). *The grain market in the Roman Empire: A social, political and economic study.* [Adobe Digital Editions version]. Retrieved from http://www.netlibrary.com/

Book: e-book (direct link to item)

Bryant, P. (1999). *Biodiversity and Conservation.* Retrieved from http://darwin.bio.uci.edu/~sustain/bio65/Titlpage.htm

Encyclopedia entry

Thomas, W. (2003). Ukulele. In *The Canadian encyclopedia of music* (Vol. 13, pp. 433–434). Vancouver, Canada: University of British Columbia Press.

Encyclopedia entry: online

Bray, K., Green, J. P., & Vogan, N. (2010). School music. In J. H. Marsh et al. (Eds.), *The Encyclopedia of music in Canada.* Retrieved from http://www.thecanadianencyclopedia.ca

Journal article: print

Jackson, J. (2005). Reconciling resource development and protection of endangered species. *New Canadian Journal of Political Science, 38*(2), 116–124.

Journal article: with DOI from online database or e-journal

Whitmeyer, J. M. (2000). Power through appointment. *Social Science Research, 29*(4), 535-555. doi:10.1006/ _ssre.2000.0680

Journal article: without DOI (include website URL)

Boutsen, F., Cannito, M. P., Taylor, M., & Bender, B. (2002). Botox treatment in adductor spasmodic dysphonia: A meta-analysis. *Journal of Speech, Language, and Hearing Research, 45*(2), 469-481. Retrieved from http://jslhr.asha.org

Magazine article

Lee, O., & Clark, L. (2003, July/August). Counting rabbits and other Victoria pastimes. *Canadian Geographic, 123*(1), 68–79.

Magazine or Journal: review

Scott, R. B. (2007). Down a familiar path [Review of the book *Harry Potter and the deathly hallows*]. *The Children's Reader, 21*(3), 47.

Newspaper article

Maverick Manitoba researcher discovers, names new planet.

(2007, June 14). *The Globe and Mail*, p. A.18.

Flores, K. E. (2000, March 7). Nursing staff key to recovery. *The New York Times*. Retrieved from http://www.nytimes.com

Website, entire

Please note: a website citation is not required in the reference list. In-text citation is sufficient.

Rules of play [Website]. (2008, March 22). Retrieved from http://www.rulesofplay.org

Web page

Gomez, D. B. (2006). A timeline of English literature. Retrieved from http://www.historyinanutshell.com/english-literature.html

Web page: no author, no date

Skunk cabbage [Web page]. (n.d.). Retrieved from http://www.wetlands.org/cabbage

Motion picture

Reed, T. (Producer), & Bell, M. (Director). (2008). *Schoolyard games* [Motion picture]. Canada: National Film Board.

Television episode

Morgan, T. (Reporter). (2008). The plague of plagiarism [Television series episode]. In Y. Barnes (Producer), *Island Pulse*.

Television series

Foster, L. (Producer). (2003-2005). *Espionage* [Television series].

Reprinted custom course materials

Powell, T. (2007). Does Canadian history matter? In K. Reyes (Ed.), *HIST 131 Course Readings* (pp. 24-37). Victoria, BC: University of Victoria, Bookstore. (Reprinted from *Journal of Western Canadian History, 42*(3), 210-223, 1984).

Podcast

Price, Y. (Producer). (2008, May 10). *Contemporary popular music culture in Shanghai.* [Audio podcast]. Retrieved from http://www.chinapop.com/music/podcasts

Blog post

Bell, L. (2009, March 25). Can students survive on Google alone? [Blog post]. Retrieved from http://www.searchinglibrarian.com/2009/03/can_students_survive.php

Video post

Sullivan, O. [origamimaster]. (2008, June 6). How to make origami [Video file]. Retrieved from http://youtube.com/w34265Z

Facebook

PostSecret. (2010a, January 7). Live PostSecret event: Spring 2010 dates & schools. [Facebook status update]. Retrieved from https://www.facebook.com/PostSecret/posts/21977955239

Twitter

PostSecret. (2010b, January 28). Author Howard Zinn dies at 87 – Washington Post #RIPHowardZinn [Tweet]. Retrieved from https://twitter.com/postsecret/status/8319691996

APPENDIX

Use an appendix to provide brief content that supplements your paper but is not directly related to your text. If you are including an appendix, refer to it in the body of your essay:

- You may have more than one appendix.
- Each appendix should deal with a separate topic.
- Each appendix must be referred to by name (aka Appendix A) in the text of the paper.
- Each appendix must be labeled with a letter (A, B, C, etc.) according to where it appears in the paper.

Made in the USA
Las Vegas, NV
02 December 2024

13148824R00017